WELCOME TO MY COUNTRY

Welcome to the
DOMINICAN REPUBLIC

Gareth Stevens Publishing
A WORLD ALMANAC EDUCATION GROUP COMPANY

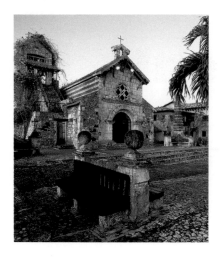

Written by
EILEEN KHOO

Edited by
MELVIN NEO

Edited in USA by
JENETTE DONOVAN GUNTLY

Designed by
GEOSLYN LIM

Picture research by
SUSAN JANE MANUEL
THOMAS KHOO

First published in North America in 2005 by
Gareth Stevens Publishing
A World Almanac Education Group Company
330 West Olive Street, Suite 100
Milwaukee, Wisconsin 53212 USA

Please visit our web site at
www.garethstevens.com
For a free color catalog describing
Gareth Stevens Publishing's list of high-quality
books and multimedia programs,
call 1-800-542-2595 (USA) or
1-800-387-3178 (Canada).
Gareth Stevens Publishing's fax: (414) 332-3567.

© **MARSHALL CAVENDISH INTERNATIONAL (ASIA)**
PRIVATE LIMITED 2005
Originated and designed by
Times Editions Marshall Cavendish
An imprint of Marshall Cavendish International (Asia) Pte Ltd
A member of Times Publishing Limited
Times Centre, 1 New Industrial Road
Singapore 536196
http://www.marshallcavendish.com/genref

Library of Congress Cataloging-in-Publication Data
Khoo, Eileen.
Welcome to the Dominican Republic / Eileen Khoo.
p. cm. — (Welcome to my country)
Includes bibliographical references and index.
ISBN 0-8368-3128-4 (lib. bdg.)
1. Dominican Republic—Juvenile literature. I. Title. II. Series.
F1934.2.K56   2005
972.93—dc22   2004054739

Printed in Singapore

1 2 3 4 5 6 7 8 9 09 08 07 06 05

PICTURE CREDITS
ANA Press Agency: 5, 16, 34
Bes Stock Photo Library: 37
Bettmann/CORBIS: 15 (bottom), 38
Steve Bly/Houserstock: 2, 26
Camera Press: 12 (top)
Chip & Rosa Maria de la Cueva Peterson:
    1, 6, 12 (bottom), 25, 39
Focus Team — Italy: 3 (center) 18, 40, 41
The Hutchison Picture Library: 43
International Photobank: cover, 3 (top), 19, 32
IPS: 15 (top), 29
Earl Kowall: 3 (bottom), 4, 7, 17, 22, 24, 28,
    33, 35, 36, 45
Lonely Planet Images: 20
Minerva Bernardino Foundation: 15 (center)
North Wind Picture Archives: 10
David Simson: 21, 23
Times Editions: 27
Topham Picturepoint: 11, 13, 14 (both)
Mireille Vautier: 8, 9, 30, 31

Digital Scanning by Superskill Graphics Pte Ltd

Contents

5   **Welcome to the Dominican Republic!**

6   **The Land**

10   **History**

16   **Government and the Economy**

20   **People and Lifestyle**

28   **Language**

30   **Arts**

34   **Leisure**

40   **Food**

42   **Map**

44   **Quick Facts**

46   **Glossary**

47   **Books, Videos, Web Sites**

48   **Index**

Words that appear in the glossary are printed in **boldface** type the first time they occur in the text.

Welcome to the Dominican Republic!

The Dominican Republic is one part of Hispaniola, which is an island located in the Caribbean area. The island was the first place Christopher Columbus landed in 1492 when he discovered the Americas. Let's explore the Dominican Republic and learn about its people!

The Flag of the Dominican Republic

On the Dominican flag, blue stands for hopes for the future. Red stands for the people who fought for freedom. White stands for peace. The image in the center is the country's official symbol.

The Land

The Dominican Republic takes up the eastern part of the island of Hispaniola. Haiti takes up the western part. The Dominican Republic covers an area of 18,810 square miles (48,730 square kilometers). The Atlantic Ocean lies to the north. The Caribbean Sea is to the south. The *cordilleras* (kohr-dee-YEH-rahs), or mountain chains, and valleys divide the land into three regions.

Below: In the Cibao Valley in the north of the Dominican Republic, people produce rum and raise cattle. They also grow tobacco and other plants.

The northern region is created by the Cordillera Septentrional and the valleys that surround it. Most of the country's best farmland is located in this region. The central region is created by the Cordillera Central. Pico Duarte, which is the country's highest peak, is located in the Cordillera Central. It stands about 10,417 feet (3,175 meters) high. The southwestern region is created by two different mountain chains, the Sierra de Neiba and the Sierra de Bahoruco.

Above:
The Dominican Republic's major rivers flow into the Atlantic Ocean or the Caribbean Sea. The longest river in the country, the Yaque del Norte, is located in the north. The river runs for about 184 miles (296 kilometers) and finally empties into the Atlantic Ocean.

Climate

In the Dominican Republic, the average yearly temperature is 78° Fahrenheit (26° Celsius). Temperatures usually do not change much in most regions, even during winter. Most of the country has a rainy season from May to November. On the northern coast, the rainy season is from November to January. Because it is in a **tropical** region, the country is often hit by very strong storms.

Below: Tall palm trees grow on one of the Dominican Republic's beautiful beaches. During the fierce **hurricanes** that have often hit the country, many buildings and ships along the coastline have been damaged or totally destroyed.

Plants and Animals

The Dominican Republic has many types of plants, including mahogany and cashew trees. It is also home to many kinds of birds, including the burrowing owl, the Hispaniolan lizard-cuckoo, and the narrow-billed tody. Many plants and animals in the country are in danger of becoming **extinct**, and efforts are being made to save them.

Above: The Isla Cabritos National Park has one of the largest populations of crocodiles in the world. The park is located on an island in the middle of Lake Enriquillo.

History

The Taino were the first people to live in what is now called the Dominican Republic. They lived on the island for as many as five thousand years before Christopher Columbus arrived in 1492. He claimed Hispaniola for the Spanish. They ruled the island for more than two hundred years. The Spanish mined gold on the island and often forced the Taino to work as slaves. Many of the Spanish later left to mine silver in Mexico.

Left: This picture shows Christopher Columbus meeting the Taino people. Under Spanish rule, many Taino were abused or killed. Many others starved to death or caught diseases brought by the Spanish. Within only fifty-six years of Spanish rule, all but five hundred Taino people had died or been killed.

The French and the Haitians

In 1697, Spain gave France the western part of Hispaniola. The French built a **colony** and brought in African slaves to help them harvest sugar. In 1795, Spain gave the rest of the island to France. In 1804, the area of the island France first ruled declared **independence**. It was then named Haiti. The Spanish took back its eastern lands in 1809. After a short period of independence, the land was taken over by the Haitians in 1822.

A Struggle for Control

From 1822 to 1844, the Haitians ruled all of Hispaniola. People in the eastern regions of the island formed a group called La Trinitaria and began to fight back. On February 27, 1844, the eastern part of the island won its independence. It was named the Dominican Republic. Freedom did not last. Harsh military leaders soon took control. In 1861, the republic's military ruler asked Spain to take over, and it did. After four years of fighting by the Dominican people, the Spanish were forced to leave again.

Below: People in eastern Hispaniola fought for freedom from Haiti in 1844. Juan Pablo Duarte, Francisco del Rosario Sanchez, and Ramon Matias Mella led the fight. Today, they are called the country's "founding fathers."

Left: In 1914, United States president Woodrow Wilson (1856–1924) told the Dominican Republic that he would send in soldiers to take control unless they held a fair election. Juan Isidro Jiménez was elected, but a powerful Dominican general tried to take him out of office. U.S. soldiers then went in and took over all large cities.

The United States Takes Over

From 1865 to 1905, the Dominican Republic suffered many problems in its government, economy, and social life. In 1905, the United States took over the country's **finances**, but the problems did not get better. Between 1916 and 1924, the United States controlled the country's government and its finances. During that time, the **political** fighting stopped, and education and services improved. In 1924, the United States pulled out of the Dominican Republic.

Many Changes in Leadership

From 1930 to 1961, Rafael Leónidas Trujillo ruled the Dominican Republic. For a short time, Joaquín Balaguer was president. After a **civil war** broke out in 1965, the United States sent in soldiers. After the war, Balaguer again became president. He controlled the results of elections and was president from 1966 to 1978 and from 1986 to 1994. He then left because people were angry over his abuse of power. In 1996, in one of the country's fairest elections, Dr. Leonel Fernandez Reyna was elected president.

Above: Rafael Leónidas Trujillo (1891–1961) ruled as a harsh **dictator**. The people of the Dominican Republic had few freedoms. Often, those who fought him were taken prisoner or killed. In 1961, the Dominican military killed Trujillo.

Left: In March 1967, Joaquín Balaguer gave a speech. He served as president many times. The first time was while Rafael Trujillo was the country's ruler. Under the rule of Trujillo, Balaguer had no real power.

Juan Pablo Duarte (1813–1876)

As the founder of La Trinitaria, Juan Pablo Duarte helped free the country from Haitian rule. He became the nation's first president but soon was forced to leave the country when General Pedro Santana took control.

Juan Pablo Duarte

Minerva Bernardino (1907–1998)

Minerva Bernardino worked hard for women's rights in the Dominican Republic and the world. She helped start a **United Nations** group to study women's lives. She also helped write a letter asking all women to take part in their government and in politics.

Minerva Bernardino

Juan Bosch (1909–2001)

In 1937, Juan Bosch, a famous writer, was forced to leave the Dominican Republic because he had written about hardships under Rafael Trujillo's rule. In 1961, Bosch came back. He became president, but after only seven months, he was taken out of office.

Juan Bosch

Government and the Economy

The Dominican government has three branches. Voters directly choose the president and vice president, who head the executive branch. They make rules for the government and also lead it. The **legislative** branch consists of the National Congress. It is made up of the Chamber of Deputies and the Senate. The Supreme Court of Justice heads the judicial branch, which runs the courts.

Below:
The National Palace is located on Doctor Ramon Baez Street in Santo Domingo, the country's capital city. The president of the Dominican Republic lives there.

Military

The military has played an important part in the country's history. When Rafael Trujillo was in power, he used the army, navy, air force, and national police to control the people. Today, to stop misuse of the military, **civilians** have been put in charge of it. Still, people do not trust the Dominican military, mainly because some military members have acted dishonestly and have been involved with drugs.

Above: Political parties put up banners beside roads and in other public places. They want to encourage people to vote for them in elections.

The Economy

In the past, most Dominicans worked on farms. Now, most of them work in industries such as tourism or finance.

In the 1980s, the government formed free trade zones. Businesses located in these areas do not pay taxes, so they are able to make more money. Many goods, including cloth and clothing, are made in these zones. In 2001, most **exports** made in the Dominican Republic were created in a free trade zone.

Below: Bananas are one of the Dominican Republic's most important crops. Sugar, tobacco, coffee, and cocoa are also important crops. Most of the crops are grown and then sold to other countries.

Tourism

Tourism is important to the Dominican Republic's economy. More and more tourists are coming from Europe and the United States to visit the country's beaches or mountains. Many also come to explore its history or culture. Others hike through the countryside and the mountains or tour caves. The most popular places to visit are towns along the coast, including Santo Domingo.

Above: Tourists often visit beaches along the coast of the Dominican Republic. Popular activities include water sports such as waterskiing, kayaking, jet skiing, and windsurfing.

People and Lifestyle

Most Dominicans have **ancestors** who were Spanish or African or a mixture of the two. These two cultures have had a great effect on the country, including its language, music, and dance. People move to the country from many places, but most of them come from Haiti. The two nations do not always get along, so most of the Haitians in the Dominican Republic are not treated well.

Left: A Dominican soldier guards the border with Haiti. The man behind him is a Haitian waiting to get into the country. During Rafael Trujillo's rule, thousands of Haitians living in the Dominican Republic were taken and killed.

Social Classes

Dominican society is made up of three levels, or classes. The "upper class" is a very small group of people. They often leave the country, make lots of money, and then return. The "middle class" is made up of people who have reliable jobs. The "lower class" is made up of people who are poor and do not have reliable jobs. More than half of all Dominicans are in the "lower class."

Above: A man in the countryside of the Dominican Republic pounds rice while sitting outside his home. Many of the Dominicans living in the countryside are poor.

Family Life

Dominican families are usually close. They depend on each other for support and help. Often, many family members live together, including grandparents, parents, and children. In those homes, the oldest man is the head of the family. In the Dominican Republic, children often have a *compadre* (kohm-PAHD-reh), or **godparent**. It is the compadre's job to help with the child's education, future career, and finances.

Below: A woman and her children relax outside their home in Santiago. Rows of tobacco leaves are hung to dry in the shade.

Dominican Women

Many Dominicans believe that women should be unselfish and always put their families first. Most women must stay at home and care for their families. They are not allowed to have jobs. Some poor women must work to survive, however. Dominican women often have a better education than men do, because some men leave school early to work. When both women and men do the same job, men are usually paid more than women.

Above: Women in the Dominican Republic usually live longer than men. Most women live an average of seventy-six years, but men only live an average of seventy-two years.

Education

Dominican children must attend school from age seven to fourteen. Then they may choose to attend a two-year course followed by secondary school, which is four years long. Even though children are supposed to attend school until they are fourteen, some cannot. They must work to help support their families.

Below:
Before Dominican students attend secondary school, they must take a two-year course.

Higher Education

After secondary school, students may attend a public or private university. The Autonomous University of Santo Domingo is entirely supported by the government. Two well-known private universities are Pedro Henríquez Ureña National University and Mother and Teacher Pontifical Catholic University. Dominican universities cost very little, so many foreign students attend them.

Above:
Students relax in front of the library on one campus of Mother and Teacher Pontifical Catholic University. There are two campuses. One is in Santiago and the other is in Santo Domingo.

Religion

Most Dominicans are Roman Catholics. Rafael Trujillo made Catholicism the Dominican Republic's official religion in 1954. In most Dominican families, Catholicism plays an important role in daily life. Other religious groups in the country include Methodists, Mormons, and Baptists. A few people are Jewish.

Below: The Church of Saint Stanislaus is located in the village of Altos de Chavón in La Romana. The village and church were built in the 1970s. They were made to look like villages built in Europe during the 1500s.

African Beliefs

Many Dominican people combine the Catholic religion with African beliefs. In the 1700s and 1800s, Yoruba people from Africa were brought as slaves to the region. They were forced to become Catholics, but they also kept their old beliefs. They combined the religions to form Santeria and Voodoo. Gagá is the Dominican form of Voodoo. It mixes Taino and African beliefs. Followers of Gagá play music and dance at services.

Above: Many adult Haitians practice Voodoo. Mainly, the religion came to the Dominican Republic when **immigrants** from Haiti moved to the country. It is also called Vodun, which comes from an African word meaning "spirit."

Language

The official language of the Dominican Republic is Spanish. Many people also speak English because of the number of Dominicans living in the United States who return for vacations. Most Haitian immigrants speak Haitian Creole, a mix of French and African languages.

Left: A sign written in Spanish points the way to a lovely waterfall. When the Spanish arrived on Hispaniola in the 1400s, they brought their language with them. Spanish is the official language of the Dominican Republic today.

Literature

The literary **tradition** of the Dominican Republic first began when the Spanish took over. Works were often written about Spanish and Haitian rule and the fight for independence. Today, many works are by Dominicans living in the United States. They often write about the hardships in their native country. Manuel de Jesus Galván (1834–1910) and Juan Bosch (1909–2001) are well-known Dominican authors. Today, Julia Alvarez is a popular Dominican writer.

Arts

Taino Art

Long before the Spanish arrived, the Taino people were creating works of art on Hispaniola. They made pottery and sculptures. They also made wood, shell, and bone decorations. Creating art was very important to the Taino. Even everyday items were decorated.

Left: A wooden Taino sculpture is displayed in a Dominican park. Many old pieces of Taino art have been found in caves or have been dug out of the ground.

Dominican Painting

In the past, Dominican painters chose traditional European subjects. Since the 1900s, they have painted subjects from Dominican history, the country's lifestyle, or from religion. Yoryi Morel and Celeste Woss y Gil are two famous artists from that time. In recent years, many Dominican paintings have been about social problems. Today, Rámon Oviedo, who paints **murals**, is one of the nation's most important painters.

Above: François J. Amiel created this colorful painting of parrots, cockatoos, and toucans in the year 2000. He is a Haitian immigrant.

Music

Dominican music is a mix of Spanish, African, and Taino styles. Dominican folk songs have many themes, including social problems and religion. *Merengue* (mehr-EN-gay) is the country's most popular music. *Bachata* (bah-CHAH-tah), a slow and soulful style of music, and salsa are also popular. Juan Luís Guerra, a famous Dominican musician, plays bachata and merengue music.

Below: Traditional merengue bands play two-sided drums, accordions, and *guiros* (WEE-rows). Guiros were Taino instruments made out of hollow gourds. Today, guiros are usually made from long metal tubes. The musician uses a special fork to rub the tube, making a scratching sound.

Dance

Most Dominicans love to dance. Many enjoy dancing the merengue, which is danced to merengue music. It has many fast steps. The merengue is the national dance of the Dominican Republic. The *sarandunga* (sah-rahn-DOONG-gah) is danced by many people at once. They dance to a guiro and three small drums. The *bolero* (bow-LEHR-row) is a dance from Spain. It is danced very slowly.

Above: Dominican women often wear long, colorful skirts when they perform folk dances.

Leisure

In the Dominican Republic, swimming and relaxing on the beach are popular. Many people also love watching sports, including **cockfighting**. Most big towns or villages have a *gallera* (gah-YEH-rah), or cockfighting pit. The sport is popular with almost all Dominicans. Horseracing is another favorite sport to watch, especially in Santo Domingo.

Below: Horseback riding is a popular leisure activity for many Dominicans. They often enjoy riding through the mountains, along beaches, and even through jungles.

Most Dominicans enjoy relaxing with family and friends. They usually meet in public parks or town squares to talk. Most women and children in the countryside go straight home after work or school. They are in charge of making dinner for the men in their households. The men often meet friends after work or on weekends to play games such as dominoes, cards, or pool.

Above:
Domino tables are very common all over the Dominican Republic. Men often play the game after work. On weekends, their games can last for many hours.

Sports

The national sport of the Dominican Republic is baseball. It was brought to the country by immigrants from Cuba. Almost every town in the country has a baseball field. Many players dream of earning lots of money by playing for teams in the United States. Several talented Dominican baseball players have achieved this dream, including Sammy Sosa and Alex Rodriguez.

Below: Dominican children often play baseball in their neighborhoods. Many Dominicans also play basketball. Tournaments are held all over the country for players as young as ten years old.

Outdoor Activities

Many Dominicans enjoy going for hikes or walks through the country's mountains, valleys, or forests or on the beaches. On February 27 each year, some brave Dominicans climb Pico Duarte to celebrate Independence Day.

Many Dominicans also enjoy fishing. They fish in places such as Samaná Bay and catch large saltwater fish, including tuna, marlin, barracuda, and sailfish.

Above:
A man shows off his catch, a barracuda. In the Dominican Republic, the best time for fishing is during the summer.

Dominican Carnival

When the Spanish came to Hispaniola, they brought the festival of Carnival. It was a religious event. Carnival is now a celebration of independence, too. Each year, there are two festivals of Carnival. The February Carnival celebrates the nation's independence from Haiti. The August Carnival honors independence from Spain. Most Dominicans take part. They wear fancy costumes and masks.

Below: Two beauty queens take part in a Carnival parade. Large groups of Dominicans watch Carnival parades. They often dance to merengue music and watch as floats covered in flowers, lively bands, and dancers parade by.

Christmas

Dominicans celebrate Christmas from December 15 to January 6. They often attend church at midnight on Christmas Eve. Most children open their presents on January 6. The night before, they put grass under their beds. They believe the Three Kings will arrive that night to see baby Jesus. The children hope that the kings' camels will eat the grass and the kings will leave presents to thank them.

Above: A woman hangs tinsel on a Christmas tree. It is common for Dominicans to go to parties and family gatherings during the long Christmas season.

Food

Food in the Dominican Republic is a mix of Taino, African, and Spanish styles of cooking. It is usually full of flavor, spice, and color.

Sancocho (sahn-KOH-choh) is the country's national dish. It is a stew of meat and vegetables. *La bandera* (lah bahn-DEH-rah) is also a popular dish. It is made of white rice, red beans, and fried green **plantains**. It is most often served with stewed meats, including chicken or beef.

Left: Roasted pork is very popular with Dominicans. They often roast a pig for special occasions, such as Christmas Eve dinner.

Snacks and Desserts

Dominicans enjoy many snacks and desserts. *Pastelitos* (pahs-teh-LEE-tohs), or meat-filled **turnovers**, and *quipes* (KEE-pehs), or fried cracked wheat and ground beef, are popular snacks. Most desserts are sweet. These include *arroz con leche* (ahr-ROHS kohn LEH-cheh), or milk and rice pudding, and *dulce de leche cortada* (DOOL-cheh deh LEH-cheh kohr-TAH-dah), or sour milk cream.

Provinces

1. Monte Cristi
2. Valverde
3. Puerto Plata
4. Espaillat
5. María Trinidad Sánchez
6. Samaná
7. Dajabón
8. Santiago Rodríguez
9. Santiago
10. La Vega
11. Salcedo
12. Duarte
13. Monseñor Nouel
14. Sánchez Ramírez
15. Monte Plata
16. Hato Mayor
17. El Seibo
18. La Altagracia
19. Elías Piña
20. San Juan
21. Azua
22. Peravia
23. San Cristóbal
24. Distrito Nacional
25. San Pedro de Macorís
26. La Romana
27. Bahoruco
28. Independencia
29. Barahona
30. Pedernales

Above: Factories that process natural gas and petroleum line the banks of the Ozama River in the Dominican Republic's capital city of Santo Domingo.

Atlantic Ocean
A1–D2

Ozama River
C2–C3

Yaque del Norte
River A1–B2

Yaque del Sur River
A3–B3

Caribbean Sea
A3–D4

Pico Duarte B2

Cibao Valley A1–B2

Puerto Plata B1

Cordillera Central
A2–B2

Cordillera
Septentrional
B1–B2

Samaná Bay C2

Santiago B2

Santo Domingo C3

Haiti A1–A3

Sierra de Bahoruco
A3–B3

La Romana D3

Lake Enriquillo A3

Sierra de Neiba
A2–A3

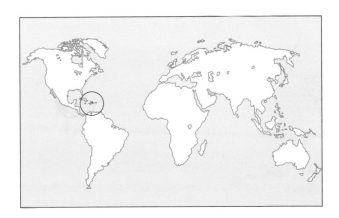

Quick Facts

Official Name   Dominican Republic

Capital   Santo Domingo

Official Language   Spanish

Population   8,715,602 (July 2003 estimate)

Land Area   18,810 square miles (48,730 square km)

Major Leaders   Juan Pablo Duarte (1813–1876)

                          Rafael Trujillo (1891–1961)

                          Joaquín Balaguer (1906–2002)

                          Juan Bosch (1909–2001)

                          President Hipólito Mejía (1941–)

Highest Point   Pico Duarte 10,417 feet (3,175 m)

Major Rivers   Yaque del Norte, Yaque del Sur

Major Lake   Lake Enriquillo

Major Highlands   Cordillera Septentrional, Cordillera Central,
                          Sierra de Neiba, Sierra de Bahoruco

Main Religions   Roman Catholicism, Santeria, Voodoo, Gagá

Currency   Dominican Peso (47.5 DOP = U.S. $1 as of 2004)

Opposite: Many people do their grocery shopping at the farmer's market in Puerto Plata.

Glossary

abusing: treating people, animals, or objects badly. The abuse often includes hitting or talking meanly.

ancestors: family members from the past, farther back than grandparents.

civil war: a war between two groups from the same country.

civilians: people in a society who are not part of the military or the police.

cockfighting: contests in which two roosters are put in a pen to fight.

colony: a village set up in one country that is controlled by another country.

dictator: a ruler who keeps complete control of a country, often by force.

exports (n): products sent out of a country to be sold in another country.

extinct: no longer existing or living.

finances: the money or funds owned by a government, business, or person.

godparent: a person who agrees, at the time of a child's baptism, to support and become responsible for him or her.

hurricanes: violent tropical storms with high winds and lots of rain.

immigrants: people who leave their own country and settle in another country.

independence: the state of being free of control by others.

legislative: relating to the law and the making of laws.

military: relating to soldiers or armed forces of some kind, or war.

murals: large pictures painted directly onto walls or ceilings.

native: belonging to a land or region by having first grown or been born there.

plantains: fruit similar to a banana. They are very common in tropical regions.

political: of or relating to the running of government, and making rules for it.

rebel: relating to fighting against a ruler or government.

tradition: idea, belief, or custom that is passed down from one generation to the next, including in literature or art.

tropical: relating to very warm and wet regions where plants grow all year.

turnovers: dough crusts stuffed with a filling and folded in half, then cooked.

United Nations: an international group with members from most countries in the world. It promotes understanding and peace and helps in the social and economic development of countries.

More Books to Read

Alex Rodriguez. Discover the Life of a Sports Star series. David Armentrout (Rourke Publishing)

Carnival. Alice K. Flanagan (Compass Point Books)

Christopher Columbus. Step into Reading series. Stephen Krensky (Random House)

Dominican Republic. Countries of the World series. Muriel L. Dubois (Bridgestone Books)

Dominican Republic. Countries series. Kate A. Conley (Checkerboard Books)

Dominican Republic. Many Cultures, One World series. Mary Englar (Blue Earth Books)

Dominican Republic. True Book series. Elaine Landau (Children's Press)

Mi Abuelita. Rebecca Newth (Will Hall Books)

Sammy Sosa Home Run Hitter. Power Players series. Rob Kirkpatrick (Rosen Publishing)

The Secret Footprints. Julia Alvarez (Alfred A. Knopf)

Videos

The Dominican Republic. (Travel America)

Dominican Republic. (Travelview Int.)

This is the Dominican Republic. (JCV Productions)

Journey of a Lifetime – in the Dominican Republic. (Director: Tom Cochrun/Ben Strout)

Off the Beaten Path: In the Dominican Republic. (Nineteenth Star)

Web Sites

dominicanrepinfo.com/index.htm

www.factmonster.com/ipka/ A0107475.html

www.latinosportslegends.com/sosa.htm

yahooligans.yahoo.com/reference/ factbook/dr/index.html

Due to the dynamic nature of the Internet, some web sites stay current longer than others. To find additional web sites, use a reliable search engine with one or more of the following keywords to help you locate information about the Dominican Republic. Keywords: *Hispaniola, merengue, Pico Duarte, Rafael Trujillo, Santo Domingo, Taino.*

Index

African 11, 20, 27, 28, 32, 40
Alvarez, Julia 29
Amiel, François J. 31
animals 9, 41
arts 30, 31
Atlantic Ocean 6, 7

Balaguer, Joaquín 14
beaches 8, 19, 34, 37
Bernardino, Minerva 15
Bosch, Juan 15, 29

Caribbean Sea 6, 7
Carnival 38
children 22, 24, 35, 36, 39
Christmas 39, 40
Cibao Valley 6
climate 8
Columbus, Christopher 5, 10
Cordillera Central 7
Cordillera Septentrional 7

dance 20, 27, 33, 38
Duarte, Juan Pablo 12, 15

economy 13, 16, 18, 19
education 13, 22, 23, 24, 25

family 22, 23, 24, 26, 35, 39
flag 5
food 40, 41
French 11, 28

government 13, 15, 16, 18, 25
Guerra, Juan Luís 32

Haiti 6, 11, 12, 20, 27, 38
Haitian 11, 12, 15, 20, 27, 28, 29, 31
Hispaniola 5, 6, 10, 11, 12, 28, 30, 38, 41
history 10-15, 17, 19, 31

Jesus Galván, Manuel de 29
Jiménez, Juan Isidro 13

L'Ouverture, Toussaint 11
La Romana 26
La Trinitaria 12, 15
Lake Enriquillo 9
land 6, 7
language 20, 28
leisure 34, 35
literature 29

Mella, Ramon Matias 12
military 11, 12, 14, 17
Morel, Yoryi 31
mountains 6, 19, 34, 37
music 20, 27, 32, 33, 38

Oviedo, Rámon 31

people and lifestyle 20–27
Pico Duarte 7, 37
plants 6, 9

Reyna, Leonel Fernandez 14
religion 26, 27, 31, 32
Rodriguez, Alex 36
Rosario Sanchez, Francisco del 12

Samaná Bay 37
Santiago 22, 25
Santo Domingo 5, 16, 19, 25, 34, 43
Sierra de Bahoruco 7
Sierra de Neiba 7
slaves 10, 11, 27
social classes 21
Sosa, Sammy 36
Spain 11, 12, 33, 38
Spanish 5, 10, 11, 12, 20, 28, 29, 30, 32, 38, 40
sports 19, 34, 36, 37

Taino 10, 27, 29, 30, 32, 40
tourism 18, 19
Trujillo, Rafael Leónidas 14, 15, 17, 20, 26

United States 13, 14, 19, 28, 29, 36

women 15, 22, 23, 33, 35
Woss y Gil, Celeste 31

Yaque del Norte 7